LATINOS IN BASEBALL

Roberto Alomar

An Authorized Biography

Norman L. Macht

Mitchell Lane Publishers, Inc.
P.O. Box 200
Childs, MD 21916-0200

LATINOS IN BASEBALL

Tino Martinez	Bobby Bonilla	**Roberto Alomar**	Pedro Martinez
Moises Alou	Sammy Sosa	Ivan Rodriguez	Carlos Baerga
Ramon Martinez	Alex Rodriguez	Vinny Castilla	Mariano Rivera

Library of Congress Cataloging-in-Publication Data

Macht, Norman L. (Norman Lee). 1929-
    Roberto Alomar / Norman Macht.
      p. cm. — (Latinos in baseball)
    Includes index.
    Summary: Discusses the personal life and professional career of the talented Puerto-Rican-born baseball player, Roberto Alomar.
      ISBN 1-883845-84-X (lib. bdg.)
      1. Alomar, Roberto, 1968– —Juvenile literature. 2. Baseball players—Puerto Rico—Biography—Juvenile literature. [1. Alomar, Roberto, 1968– . 2. Baseball players. 3. Puerto-Ricans—Biography.] I. Title. II. Series.
GV865.A2A566 1999
796.357'092—dc21
    [b]   98-48048
                                                                                           CIP
                                                                                           AC

About the Author: Norman Macht is the author of more than 20 books, including **The Composite Guide to Baseball** (Chelsea House). He is also the coauthor of biographies of former ballplayers Dick Bartell and Rex Barney, and is a member of the Society for American Baseball Research. He is the president of Choptank Syndicate, Inc. and lives in Baltimore, Maryland.

Photo Credits: cover: Reuters/Archive Photos/Ron Kuntz; pp. 4, 7 Reuters/Corbis-Bettmann; pp. 22, 30 Kirk Schlea/Allsport; p. 27 Barbara Bowen/Allsport; p. 36 Reuters/Corbis-Bettmann; p. 38 Reuters/Phil Snel/Archive Photos; p. 41 Rick Stewart/Allsport; p. 47 Reuters/Joe Giza/Archive Photos; pp. 48, 49, 50, 61 Jerry Wachter; p. 53 Archive Photos

Acknowledgments: The following story was developed based on personal interviews with Roberto Alomar during the 1998 baseball season. The author met with Roberto on April 27, May 18, June 21, and July 11, 1998, for the sole purpose of developing this book. Professional and personal friends and family members were also interviewed for this book: Luis Mayoral–May 20, 1998; Sandy Alomar Sr.–May 29, 1998; Sandy Alomar Jr.–May 13, 1998; Paul Molitor–May 1, 1998; and Larry Bowa–April 27–28, 1998. The final version was approved for print by Roberto Alomar. This story has been thoroughly researched and checked for accuracy. This is the story of Roberto Alomar's life—as he sees it. This is Robbie's story.

TABLE OF CONTENTS

Roberto Alomar runs down the 1st baseline with his arms in the air after he hit a two-run home run in the ninth inning against the Oakland Athletics off relief pitcher Dennis Eckersley on October 11, 1992.

CHAPTER ONE
Winning It All

The outlook wasn't very bright for the Toronto Blue Jays on a sunny Sunday October 11, 1992, in Oakland. Even though they had come into Game 4 of the American League (AL) Championship Series leading two games to one, they carried a monkey on their backs that grew larger when the A's took a 5-1 lead after three innings.

The Blue Jays had won the AL East three times and just missed three times since 1985, but they had yet to make it to the World Series. In 1985 they had blown a three-games-to-one lead against Kansas City, losing the last two at home. In 1989 the Oakland A's had dominated them in five. And just the year before, in 1991, despite the addition of Roberto Alomar, Devon White, and Joe Carter, the Minnesota Twins had dusted them off just as quickly.

"The Jays will choke again," the critics said. "They can't win the big ones." But this 1992 team didn't want to hear about being haunted by the ghosts of Blue Jays past. "That wasn't us," they said.

Still, the scene was beginning to look familiar to those who had been in some of those losing efforts when the A's batted around and scored five runs in the third inning off their pitching ace Jack Morris. Oakland added a run in the sixth and led 6-1 after seven innings.

Not only their own reputation but baseball history was against the Blue Jays. No team had ever trailed by five runs in the eighth inning and come back to win in postseason play. And the A's had been 81-1 in games in which they led after eight innings that year.

Roberto Alomar wasn't thinking about those statistics when he stepped into the batter's box to lead off the eighth. He already had two hits off A's starter Bob Welch, and he was confident of what he thought Welch would throw. He got the pitch he was looking for and lined a double. Two more hits followed, and the A's called on pitcher Dennis Eckersley to put out the fire. Eck, the greatest reliever in the game, had chalked up 51 saves and 7 wins during the season. But singles by John Olerud and Candy Maldonado made the score 6-4 before Eckersley got the next three men to end the inning. When he struck out Ed Sprague for the third out, Eckersley pumped his fist in the air and glared into the Toronto dugout. Eck was an emotional pitcher who frequently made such gestures, but Jack Morris called it "Little League stuff" and it sent sparks flying among the Jays.

Devon White led off the ninth for the Jays with a double. That brought up Alomar as the potential tying run. Back home in Salinas, Puerto Rico, his mother and sister watched on television, as did just about everyone else on the island. His mother prayed to God to "please help my son." His father, Sandy Alomar Sr., a former major-league player, sat in the Oakland Coliseum surrounded by noisy A's fans. Roberto's brother, Sandy Jr., a catcher for the Cleveland Indians, watched on TV in Cleveland.

The count went to 2-2; Alomar set himself to protect the plate. Eckersley threw a fastball. Alomar swung just to make contact. But as soon as he hit it he knew it was gone. He lifted both arms high in the air; Eck's emotional gestures were contagious.

"I don't like to show anybody up," Alomar said later. "I was just happy."

But the game was not over. Alomar's home run had tied it. The Jays loaded the bases with two out but failed to score again.

"Defense wins games," Alomar believed, and his glove had made a difference in this game as well as his bat. He had been in the middle of two key double plays that cut short Oakland threats. He was about to be tested again.

Oakland's Harold Baines led off the bottom of the ninth with a base hit. Pinch-runner Eric Fox stole second. Mark McGwire sacrificed Fox to third. With one out, a fly ball could plate the winning run and even the series.

Toronto manager Cito Gaston faced a decision: to walk the bases full and set up a force or possible double

On October 10, 1992, Roberto Alomar connected for a solo home run during the 4th inning of game 3 of the ALCS against the Oakland Athletics. The catcher was Terry Steinbach.

play, or pitch to Terry Steinbach with the infield pulled in. He chose to pitch to Steinbach, who hit a ground ball to second. Alomar scooped it up and fired home to get the speedy Fox by 10 feet.

In the top of the 11th the Jays put together a walk, a single, and a sacrifice fly to score the winning run—after 4 hours 25 minutes.

Oakland won Game 5, 6-2, and the series went back to Toronto, where the Blue Jays lost no time in nailing down their first pennant. In the top of the first, Alomar made a sensational play on a ball hit over second base by Jerry Browne. He grabbed it, leaped high, and threw the runner out at first. In the bottom of the first he singled and scored on Joe Carter's home run. Alomar had three hits and two stolen bases in the Jays' 9-2 win.

Alomar batted .423 with two home runs, four RBIs, and five stolen bases and won the ALCS Most Valuable Player Award. The Blue Jays went on to win the World Series over the Atlanta Braves.

In the years that followed, Roberto Alomar had many more big games, outstanding seasons, and individual honors. But looking back he said, "That Game 4 in 1992 is still my biggest game because we were ahead two games to one, but if they had won they would have evened the series. They won the next day, so it would have been 3-2 with them ahead in the playoffs. That day I had four hits, hit a home run to tie it in the ninth, stole two bases, and made some great defensive plays to help give my team a lift and one more step to the World Series. I had some big games in other playoffs when we didn't go all the way. That's why I say for me this was my biggest game."

For Roberto Alomar, baseball was his life, but winning was its purpose.

CHAPTER 2
Born to Play Baseball

Roberto Alomar y Velasquez was born on February 5, 1968, to Santos and Maria Velasquez Alomar in Ponce, Puerto Rico. (In the Spanish custom, his mother's maiden name was added to his father's name, but it would not be used.) The family, which included a sister, Sandia, born July 4, 1965, and a brother, Santos Jr., born June 18, 1966, lived in nearby Salinas, a small town on the south coast of the island. Only 40 miles from the capital, San Juan, Salinas was separated by lush green mountains that made it seem like another world.

Roberto was born into the premier baseball family of Puerto Rico. His father, known as Sandy, then a second baseman for the Chicago White Sox, would play 15 years in the major leagues. Three of Roberto's uncles played professional baseball, all of them starring in the Puerto Rico Winter League. The warm climate enabled the islanders to play ball all year, but winter was the best time, when local heroes came home from the major leagues to play before their friends and neighbors, and other big-league stars performed as well on local diamonds from November to February.

Puerto Rican baseball "fanaticos" are as avid rooters for their favorite teams as any fans in the States. They idolize their homegrown former stars like Roberto Clemente and Orlando Cepeda, and current stars like the Alomars and Juan Gonzalez, just as Baltimore fans worship Cal Ripken Jr. and fans everywhere adore the grinning Ken Griffey Jr. The annual Caribbean World Series, which involves teams from Venezuela, Mexico, Puerto

Rico, and the Dominican Republic, rivals the major leagues' World Series for intensity and fan interest.

Robbie Alomar sprouted baseball talent quicker than he cut teeth. As soon as he could walk he carried a glove and bat and ball wherever he went. When he was six a scout saw him playing pepper and asked his father, "Can I sign him now?"

The Alomars were a very close family, but as in most baseball families, the mother bore the brunt of the child-rearing. "It was tough on her with my dad away in the States playing ball," Roberto recalled. "He called home every day, but it was not easy for her to raise three kids almost by herself. She gave us love and direction, the main things you need to grow up right. I never went wrong following the advice of my mother or father. We never used drugs or alcohol. I have never smoked or chewed tobacco. To be successful in baseball or anything in life, you should try to stay away from those things. I have done it. Anyone else can, too."

Robbie's mother was helped by Grandma Toni, who lived nearby. "My mother and her sisters had been raised from infancy by this woman. We used to go to her house all the time. She cooked and did things for us. Whenever my mother had to go away we would stay with her. She was more than a grandmother to me; she was a friend I could talk to. If I went out with a girl and she didn't like the girl, she would tell me, 'That girl's not for you,' and I listened to her. She was always looking out for what was best for me."

When school was over the family joined Sandy wherever he was playing for the summer. Roberto's earliest memory is when he was five and his father was with the California Angels. Sandy Sr. spent the next three years with the Yankees. On the field and in the clubhouse, Robbie and his brother absorbed big-league behavior and attitudes.

"I remember playing in the clubhouse with Barry Bonds. We would crunch a paper cup for a ball and use a stick or our hand to hit it. When the players were in there, we always did what our father said. If they lost, we stayed out of the clubhouse. When we were in there, we would sit in Dad's locker and not move. We respected the players' privacy and didn't bother them. But sometimes they talked to us.

"In California, Nolan Ryan taught me how to pitch. In New York, Catfish Hunter, Craig Nettles, and Carlos May were nice to us.

"I loved being in there among all those big-league players, and dreamed of being one of them someday. At school in the fall the other kids would ask me how the players were as people. Many fans don't realize that players are not the same on and off the field. Yankees' catcher Thurman Munson had a reputation for being grumpy. But he was very friendly with us. When a player is in the game, he has an intensity, doing things to win. But after the game he is back to normal. A lot of fans judge us just by what they see on the field or what they read about us, and that's not what we are really like as people."

After the 1978 season in Texas, Sandy Sr. was released. He could have taken a minor-league or traveling job in baseball, but his kids were getting bigger and his wife welcomed some help in raising them. He stayed in Salinas, played in the winter league, and bought a gas station.

To 10-year-old Robbie, that was the wrong decision. His summers in big-league clubhouses were over. He begged his father not to retire, to no avail.

But Robbie still had his winters with his dad in baseball, where Sandy Sr. played and managed. His father had not been a high-paid star in the major leagues, but he was a hero in the winter league. One of the few players who reached 1,000 hits in his winter-league career, he won the batting championship in 1970–71, a title Robbie would also win 25 years later.

It was a long, hard drive, some of it over narrow curving mountain roads, to San Juan or other cities where the games were played. Robbie insisted on going with his father, running home from school to get there before his father left. He sobbed for hours if he was too late. Once when he was told to stay home he hid behind the front seat and didn't show himself until it was too late to turn back. It was often past midnight when they got home. Robbie slept in the car, but he still had a hard time getting up for school the next morning. His mother had to start dressing him and feeding him his breakfast while he was still in bed. When his father dropped out of baseball for a few years, Robbie went to the games with the broadcaster for a local radio station.

Sometimes Sandy Jr. went with them. They played in the outfield, took infield grounders, got in some batting practice when they could pester somebody into pitching for them, and played in the clubhouse during the game. Robbie often sat in the dugout and did his homework. School meant less to him than baseball, but his mother laid down the law: "If you don't make good grades, you don't play baseball."

Sandy Sr. talked baseball with the boys at home and at the ballpark. He taught them how to behave in a big-league way. When the boys got out of line, he set them straight with an explanation, not a wallop.

Longtime Puerto Rican sportswriter and broadcaster Luis Mayoral knew the family. "Sandy Sr. was a very disciplined player who took pride in the way he wore his uniform. The way Roberto carries himself on and off the field came from his dad."

Of the two boys, Robbie had the more single-minded dedication to baseball. They could have banned the game on the island and he would have found a way to play it in the ocean. Sandy Jr. was into everything: model airplanes, remote control cars, volleyball, go-carts, motorcycles. Robbie was the quiet one; Sandy did all the talking. He made the friends, while Robbie tagged along shyly.

Once Sandy scared the daylights out of him. Robbie was riding behind his brother on the motorcycle. Sandy roared up a mountainside and leaped the bike over a big hole. That was enough biking for Robbie.

Like most brothers, the boys fought sometimes, especially when they played competitive games. No matter what it was, Robbie had to win. His love for baseball was matched by his hatred for losing. He would rather cheat than lose, and that made Sandy mad. Robbie didn't think of it as cheating; to him, he was just doing whatever it took to win.

"At that time I didn't know what losing was all about," he said later. "One time I was playing shortstop in a Little League game and I wanted to pitch because I thought we could win if I pitched. But the manager wouldn't let me. I didn't like that and I pouted and made a fuss. My dad was in the stands. He knew the best way to punish me; he told the manager to take me out of the game, and out I went."

The family's income dropped when Sandy Sr.'s playing days ended. There were financial problems. Some investments went bad. He loaned money that was not repaid. Robbie did not know all the details, but he watched and learned and vowed never to be so loose and easy with his money, long before he had earned any.

Robbie earned $25 a week working for a neighbor, Nestor Pabon, who owned a pharmacy in Salinas. Robbie kept the store clean and did odd jobs. Pabon allowed the Alomar boys to use his beachhouse to go swimming and boating with his daughters. "He taught me how to be a good human being," Robbie said. "He helped me when my dad was away."

Luis Munoz High School in Salinas had no baseball team, but the students played softball. When the boys played on different Little League and American Legion teams, their mother would take Sandy to one park, Robbie to another, and go back and forth trying to watch them both play at the same time. Later, when they were both in the major leagues, she had a split-screen TV to watch them.

Seeing big-league games on television, Robbie admired Pete Rose and second baseman Joe Morgan because they played the game so aggressively. But his dad remained his idol. "I played shortstop, second base, and pitched growing up," he recalled. "I moved to second base because I wanted to be like my dad, although he played every position except pitcher and catcher in the big leagues. He had started his career wearing the number one, so I wanted to wear that number." Sandy Sr.'s career had gotten a big boost when he had become a switch-hitter. He suggested that Robbie do the same.

"I was a natural right-handed hitter," Robbie said. "But I followed his advice from the start. I hit a lot left-handed because all they had in Little League was right-handed pitchers. I had a lot of practice."

He learned to lose—but never to like it—when his team went outside Salinas. "It was a small town. My team won all the time there, but against other teams in Puerto Rico, we didn't do very well."

As Robbie grew, his father's view of his potential grew also. At 13, Robbie was still an immature boy, but he already had major-league mental and physical tools. He could go hitless in a game and remain confident that he would get his hits the next day. On defense he was taking the chances and making the plays that would become fare for highlight films a decade later. From the beginning, his father said, "he was never afraid of making a mistake."

That didn't mean it all came easily to him. "Nothing came easy to me," Robbie said. "It came naturally. I feel gifted. God gave me a talent, but it was up to me to practice every day to become the player I would be."

Robbie was 16 when he signed his first professional contract with Caguas in the Puerto Rico Winter League. "It was 45 minutes from my home, but sometimes we played away games and I had to drive maybe two hours after school to get there. Then I had to drive home that night after the game and get up for school the next morning."

Felipe Alou, a major-league star, was the Caguas manager. "Alomar could do everything," Alou recalled. "He could run, field, hit, turn a double play. I managed a lot of young players, but he was the best I had ever seen. He was a natural and definitely had the instincts that you just don't teach." Later, as manager of the Montreal Expos, Alou would equate Alomar with Puerto Rican hero Roberto Clemente and other Baseball Hall of Famers Willie Mays and Hank Aaron, as one of the few "who have a special gift."

CHAPTER 3
Minor League Life

Major-league scouts had watched Roberto Alomar grow up playing Little League, American Legion, and winter-league ball. They knew his father's reputation for discipline and hard work and saw it rub off on Robbie and his brother. As eagerly as kids awaiting Christmas, they counted the days until they could sign him.

In October 1983 Sandy Jr. had signed with San Diego scout Luis Rosa, a friend of the family, and gone to Spokane, Washington, in the Northwest League. Their father was then a coach in the Padres' organization. Watching the Padres in the 1984 World Series, Robbie announced his intention to play for them; he dreamed of hitting the winning home run in the ninth inning.

Sandy Sr. had given Luis Rosa his word that Robbie was his. Despite offers of higher bonuses, particularly from Toronto, Sandy Sr. kept his word and signed a Padres contract for his son on February 16, 1985, 11 days after Robbie turned 17. Robbie never saw the bonus money of about $50,000; his father put it safely away in a savings account.

Roberto had an advantage denied most minor-league rookies: his whole family, except for his sister, went with him. His father was a coach and his brother was the catcher for the Class A Charleston, South Carolina, team in the South Atlantic League, where he was assigned. His mother cooked and took care of the family. Robbie saw other young players, alone and away from home for the first time, get so homesick they dropped out, despite their talent.

Robbie had another edge over most young Latin players. Spanish-speaking teenagers suddenly on their own in a different culture with a different language have a tough time dealing with everyday life. If there were no other Latinos on the team, they had nobody to talk to. Unable to read a menu, they often went hungry, or they ate the first thing they learned to order at every meal. They might wind up with eggs and spaghetti for breakfast, or eating liver at every meal. Robbie had taken English classes in school, but he had learned more by talking to people during the summers spent in the States when his father was playing.

Many rookies, used to playing two or three games a week, are unable to cope with the grind of playing almost every day over a 137-game schedule. But Robbie loved it. "He took off for me," recalled his manager, Jim Skaalen. "He was tearing up the league against older college players. Outgoing and friendly, he had a lot of fun and was full of enthusiasm."

Alomar batted .293, averaging more than one hit per game, and stole 36 bases.

"He could drag a bunt, hit to all fields," Skaalen said. "Solid in the field with no flaws. Batting right-handed, his swing got long at times. As a left-hander, his swing was always short and compact." (A long swing means the bat is looping down and then up under the hands, or it is going out and around, instead of a short, straight swing.)

But having his father as a coach was a mixed blessing. "Robbie put pressure on himself to excel and tried to do too much," Skaalen said. "He had high expectations for himself. When he would mess up, or when I or his father would say something harsh to him, you could see the tears in his eyes. He would get discouraged at umpires who missed calls on him. But he was playing with a passion and intensity that it takes to make it to the major leagues and succeed there."

Things were different in 1986 when Robbie found himself alone in Reno, Nevada, in the Class A California League, thousands of miles from home in an erratic climate without his family. His father was a coach with the Padres at the time. His brother was with Beaumont in the Texas League. He saw snow for the first time—during batting practice. It could be 75 degrees one day and snowing the next. But the cold weather was not his biggest adjustment.

"In the minor leagues everything is different. I was making $700 a month. I had to pay for rent, utilities, food, clubhouse dues. All I had in the house I rented was a mattress on the floor, not even a table. I had no car and had to walk everywhere.

"There was no hot water in the clubhouse. After a game you had to get back into your clothes and go home to take a shower and go to sleep. Next day you wake up, get a hamburger, go to the ballpark and work.

"On the road you wake up about noon. You and your roommate go and eat some fast food, go back and change into your uniform in the motel room, and get on the bus at four o'clock. The trainer did the laundry. You wore a T-shirt and your game pants for batting practice, then put on the game shirt. After the game you hope to find a fast-food place still open. If you don't, you get a bag of chips or something and go to sleep hungry until the next day.

"You feel like you want to go back home, like, 'This is not the life I want to lead.' But if you have the dream and you know this is what you have to do to make it come true, you stick it out. Later, when you are in the big leagues, you can look back and say it all paid off. It was worth it. But at the time you have to be strong enough mentally to keep working at it.

"You realize you have to work hard. There is a lot of competition—other guys with the same dream you have—and you don't want to be in the minor leagues any longer than you have to. Whenever there is an opening in the big leagues, maybe you can be the guy to go up there and show them you deserve to be there. I know it's easy to say, but it's not easy to do."

Jim Skaalen, who had moved from Charleston to Reno as manager, saw a change in Roberto. "He seemed more relaxed away from his dad and brother. He got stronger and seemed to be enjoying every day. He was far ahead of the rest of the talent at that level, and I began to see the good, solid, major-league player he was going to become."

Reno was different from most minor-league towns. In Nevada gambling is legal, and Reno was filled with casinos and nightclubs. "In addition to the normal problems you have with young players on their own for the first time," Skaalen said, "in Reno a few kids lost their paychecks gambling and would hit up other players for money."

The problem was worse for visiting teams; in Reno for just a few days, their players might lose their meal money and some sleep gambling, to the home team's advantage.

Robbie led the league by batting .346 with 123 hits in 90 games, and he cut his errors in half to 18. That earned him a promotion to Wichita, Kansas, in the AA Texas League, where he was reunited with Sandy Jr.

Some things were better in Wichita than in Reno. It didn't snow. Robbie was making $1,200 a month and shared a one-bedroom apartment with his brother. They had one bed and a couch and took turns sleeping on the bed. They bought a car for $300 and lived on fast food and pizza.

But the bus rides were torturous. Ten- or 12-hour treks were routine after playing a night game. They slept on the bus floor, the seats, the equipment bags—and had to play the next day. In the major leagues, players tend to go their own way, but the shared discomfort on the buses promoted a closeness and made it necessary to be able to get along with others.

"You had to go through all that pain to see if you could make it to the big leagues," Alomar said. "It was like going to school. You have to graduate before you can go to the big leagues."

The Wichita manager was Steve Smith, a veteran minor-league infielder who helped Roberto go from good to great that year. Smith worked with him on his footwork in turning a double play, on the art of reading pitchers to steal bases, on bunting—all the little parts of the game that add up to winning. He was impressed by Robbie's complete self-confidence.

"Roberto didn't care if it was a one-run lead or 10-run lead in the eighth inning, he performed. He was a clutch player, never scared in tough situations. At El Paso in the division playoffs, Sandy hit a home run, then Roberto hit the game-winning double in the ninth to put us in the finals. He just numbed out everything and saw the ball and hit it. To look at him you couldn't tell if he was swinging in batting practice or in the World Series. You still can't tell."

The brothers were very close and looked out for each other. At one stage of the season, Smith thought the team was dogging it a little bit. "We were in Jackson, Mississippi. I called a meeting in the clubhouse, which was not much bigger than a closet. Everybody was squashed in together. We had just come off one of those long bus rides and the guys were a little irritable.

"There are some players you can get on to use as an example to get the others pumped up, and some you can't. Robbie was sensitive, but Sandy had played for me for a few years. I knew I could get in his face and he could take it, and he would know why I was doing it.

"'You're not working as hard as you should,' I barked at him in the meeting. 'You've got to get it together.'

"Roberto was offended. He jumped in front of Sandy and said, 'Don't you yell at my brother like that.'

"I said, 'Roberto, sit down.' Sandy grabbed him and moved him away.

"It worked. It got the guys fired up. We went on to win the league championship against Jackson."

That year Roberto hit .319 with 41 doubles and 12 home runs. He ran up 43 stolen bases. Today he credits Skaalen and Smith and others for his growth. "I learned from everybody who helped me along the way and [from] some who didn't realize they were helping me when I watched how they did things. They all helped me be where I am now, and I'm grateful to them."

The Alomar brothers went with their father to the Padres' training camp in the spring of 1988. Robbie believed he had proven himself in the minor leagues. The Padres' second base job was up for grabs and he was determined to earn it. The equipment man handed him a uniform with the number 67 on it. "Man, this is a big number," Robbie thought. "I know for sure I'm going back to the minors now." His dad had started his career wearing number 1. Robbie had worn it in the winter league. He said to the equipment man, "How about number one?"

In 1989, the Alomars were all affiliated with the San Diego Padres. From left to right: Sandy Sr., Roberto, and Sandy Jr.

That was shortstop Garry Templeton's number, and he had been in the big leagues for 12 years. So that was out. Robbie's dad had worn number 2 and was still wearing it. Robbie decided to combine them.

"How about 12?" he asked.

Twelve was available; he took it and stayed with it from then on.

Larry Bowa, the San Diego manager, was a shortstop whose 16-year career included six National League Championship Series and one World Series with the Phillies. Bowa held the record for career fielding average by a shortstop—.980. So he knew what he was talking about when he looked at the 20-year-old Alomar and said,

"This kid is a finished product. All he has to do is go out there and play. He has all the tools; just turn him loose."

Bowa recognized Sandy Sr.'s influence. "The way he played and approached the game, Roberto was taught right. He had the most poise of any young kid I'd ever seen in his first year in a big-league camp. Unlike most rookies, he was not in awe of anybody. He'd step in against big-league pitchers like he'd been doing it for years. You knew he was something special."

Robbie backed up Bowa's first impressions. In the early exhibition games he made diving stops, turned double plays, and stole bases. He had the highest batting average on the team. Bowa considered his second base problem solved, not just for the 1988 season, but for many years to come. Batting champion Tony Gwynn watched Alomar at the plate and said, "He's going to make the club."

The night before cut-down day, while Robbie enjoyed the sleep of the confident, an argument about him raged. Larry Bowa wanted to keep him; the club's general manager, Jack McKeon, wanted to send him back to the minors. Through the night and into the early hours of morning they fought.

"He's the best player we've got," Bowa argued. "He's done everything we've asked of him."

"He's going down," McKeon insisted, without ever offering a reason.

The next morning Bowa sat in his office with Robbie's dad. "Sandy," he said, "I can't look at him and tell him there's a reason to send him down. I'll just have to be honest with him."

When Robbie came in, Bowa recalled, "I had trouble looking him in the eye and telling him that he wasn't good enough to make the team. In my mind and in my heart I knew he was. It felt like I was lying to him, yet I was trying to be honest with him.

"'We're sending you down to Las Vegas,' I said, 'and don't ask me why. I don't know why. I guess it's for experience. You're the best infielder we have. You made the team as far as I'm concerned.'

"It was the hardest thing I ever had to do as a manager in the big leagues."

Alomar was disappointed, but the tears that wet his face poured from a bigger, darker cloud than mere disappointment. He was angry and frustrated to realize that all the talent, hard work, and determination in the world had not earned him the promotion he felt he deserved.

Steve Smith was then the manager at Las Vegas. "When they sent him down he was shocked," Smith recalled. "He thought the world was going to end. When he reported to me I sat and talked to him for a half hour, telling him how I had spent four years as a Triple-A shortstop because the Padres had Ozzie Smith in front of me, and how he'd be back up there in no time. I never got up there and I'm looking at this 20-year-old kid and thinking, 'So they sent you down. Most kids would say okay, I'll be back soon.' But he was devastated."

Sandy Jr. had been sent to Las Vegas and was sharing an apartment with second baseman Joey Cora. Sandy invited his brother to move in with them, telling him, "With your talent, you'll only be here a short time."

Robbie made up his mind to work hard and play so well they couldn't keep him down for long. "I had 10 hits and 14 RBIs and three stolen bases in nine games and they called me back up, and that was the last time I spent in the minor leagues."

CHAPTER 4
Making the Plays

A smiling, confident Roberto Alomar strode into the San Diego clubhouse at Jack Murphy Stadium on April 22, 1988. He was in a place where he knew he belonged. He had felt at home in big-league clubhouses, around the greatest players, since he was six years old.

It didn't even faze him that he would be making his major-league debut batting against the legendary Nolan Ryan of the Houston Astros. Veterans enjoyed teasing rookies facing Ryan for the first time, telling them how Ryan would stand on the mound grunting and glaring at them before firing a 100-mile-an-hour heater an inch under their chin.

But Robbie heard none of that and, besides, it wouldn't have bothered him. To him, that was just good old "Uncle Nolie" out there, someone who had played with him and taught him how to pitch when Ryan and Sandy Sr. had been teammates with the California Angels.

Coaching at third base, Sandy Sr. was more nervous than his 20-year-old son when Robbie stepped into the batter's box to face the 41-year-old Ryan. "I wasn't nervous," Robbie recalled. "I was having fun. He didn't intimidate me. The pitcher would love for you to be intimidated, but you have to be strong mentally and hang in there. If I had been scared I would have stayed home. I just went up to swing the bat and get on base any way I could."

Batting left-handed, Robbie worked the count to 2 and 2. Ryan threw a curve that hung up enough for Robbie to drill it between third and short. The third baseman dove for it and stopped it, but he had no play. Sandy Sr. retrieved the ball and it wound up in the trophy case in the Alomar family home in Salinas. Robbie capped his debut by completing a sparkling double play in the ninth to help save a victory for the Padres.

Alomar faced other pitchers he had watched when his dad was playing, and he knew how they worked and what to expect from them. But a week after hitting his first home run on April 30, he went into a two-week slump and was benched for the first time. He didn't like sitting, but the day off proved to be good for him and he came back hitting again.

Robbie was eager to show everybody what he could do. He dove after and caught ground balls and line drives that nobody expected him to catch. Then he would throw off-balance, the ball sometimes sailing into the outfield. On routine grounders, infielders are taught to get in front of the ball if they can, plant their back foot, and wing it. But that was not Robbie's style. He preferred to reach to his side for it and flip it softly to first.

He pulled off some spectacular plays that raised goose bumps on his father. In one game he stopped a ball behind second base and threw out the runner from his knees. The next man up hit an identical drive. This time Robbie slid across the grass to stop it, popped up, and got his man.

"It looked like he was being nonchalant," said Tony Gwynn. Some players called him lazy. Then the media started talking about it, and that got the fans down on him. They ignored the fact that he was getting to balls that other infielders wouldn't even try for, and they didn't understand that his talent was what made it look so easy. Instead they accused him of hotdogging.

Outfielder Joe Carter understood Alomar. "He was full of energy and he had the talent, so when he got in front of all those people in the stands he wanted to show off what he could do. A lot of young players do that. You want people to notice you. I did it myself in high school and college. Until you prove yourself, criticism just comes with the territory."

But the criticism bothered Roberto. "I was only 20, in my first year in the big leagues. When writers say things about you and fans get on you, you don't know how to take it. It took a long time for me to learn about the media and the fans. As I got more mature I realized that as long as you go out there and do the best you can, you cannot worry about what comes at you from outside."

Robbie also carried

In this photo taken in 1990, Roberto was just 22 years old.

the same burden as other sons of ballplayers, like Barry Bonds and Ken Griffey Jr. "That was the hardest thing for me. People think because you're the son of a player, you should do everything right from day one. I didn't do everything right from the beginning. I made a lot of mistakes like anybody else. People didn't expect that."

Alomar enjoyed playing for manager Larry Bowa, who had fought for him to stay with the big club in the spring. He appreciated Bowa's honesty and directness; a person knew where he stood with him. He didn't say one thing to someone and something else behind his back. Bowa was a throwback to the days when managers yelled at players for making mental mistakes and not going all out all the time, the way he had played. Robbie played as hard and aggressive a game as Bowa ever did, and he was left alone. Off the field Robbie was quiet and respectful, watching and listening and learning.

But others in the organization did not care for Bowa's style. The Padres had finished last in the National League West in 1987 and were faring no better in early 1988. Bowa was fired, and Jack McKeon, the general manager who had ordered Alomar's return to the minors in the spring, replaced him.

Alomar was a big factor in the Padres' strong finish to reach third place that year. He put together three hitting streaks of at least 10 games in August and September and led the team in runs and doubles. His 16 sacrifices topped all non-pitchers in the league. He stayed sharp by playing in the winter league back home and showed up at spring training in Arizona with a $155,000 contract and a lock on the second base job. At 21, he was still the youngest player in the major leagues on opening day.

The Padres had high hopes for the 1989 season. They had added slugging first baseman Jack Clark to a dazzling middle infield of Alomar and shortstop Garry Templeton, all-star catcher Neito Santiago, and perennial batting champion Tony Gwynn, who would win his third consecutive batting title. They almost won the West, finishing three games behind San Francisco.

Hitting safely in 31 of the last 33 games, Alomar wound up at .295. He was third in hits with 184, tied for second with 42 stolen bases, and—thanks to his bunting skill—first in sacrifices with 17. But he also led all keystone sackers (second basemen) with a whopping 28 errors.

Fielders who cover the most ground often make the most errors, because they get to balls that others would just wave at as they went by. But to some observers, Robbie still seemed too aggressive and undisciplined in the field. He was everywhere, charging balls he should have stayed back on, diving to stop drives far to his left or right, then throwing when he had no chance to get the runner instead of sticking it in his pocket.

The media critics got on him, but that didn't make him change his style. "I didn't care what they said. I made mistakes, but I was learning from my mistakes."

The Padres asked Alomar to take the winter off; for the first time since he had broken in at 17, he did not play in the Puerto Rico Winter League.

The arrival of Joe Carter in San Diego in 1990 helped Robbie mature as a player, and a longtime friendship began between them. At 30, Carter was an established leader. He immediately saw Alomar as a special talent who was still making a lot of young mistakes. Carter talked to him about things like knowing the right time to try to steal a base instead of running wild, regardless of the situation.

The Padres were still a sub-.500 team in June when manager Jack McKeon benched Garry Templeton and switched Alomar to shortstop. Roberto had played short for a while at Wichita, but he considered second base his natural position. Soon after that, McKeon resigned and coach Greg Riddoch replaced him. The change cost Sandy Sr. his coaching job. For the first time, Robbie was alone

Sandy Sr. with Roberto in 1989

in the big leagues. He would have to rely on the telephone to get his father's counsel.

The highlight of the season was Robbie's first All-Star Game, played at Wrigley Field in Chicago. It was even more special because his brother made the American League All-Star team. Sandy, who had spent more time in the minors than Roberto, had been traded to the Cleveland Indians, where he was on his way to winning the

Rookie of the Year Award as the Indians' catcher. Their proud parents were on hand to share the big day, and everyone in Puerto Rico took great pride in their All-Star Alomars.

When the regular season resumed, Robbie told the new manager he did not want to play shortstop. Riddoch reluctantly agreed to return him to second base. Alomar was uncomfortable playing for Riddoch, who accused him of not having his head in the game and who bad-mouthed him to the press. This upset Sandy Sr., who knew his son had no problems on or off the field.

Robbie made only six errors in the second half of the season and was fast becoming a favorite of the San Diego fans. The Padres had another losing record, but Alomar saw evidence that they were building a winner. He and Joe Carter were assured that they were important parts of the Padres' future. Robbie bought a house in San Diego. Carefree and contented, he went with an all-star team to Japan after the season.

Alomar was asleep one morning in December when the phone rang. It was his agent, calling to tell him that he and Joe Carter had been traded to the Toronto Blue Jays in the American League East. Stunned, confused, and scared of the unknown—"I didn't expect it; I didn't understand it"—he called his parents in Salinas.

His father tried to convince him that Toronto was a first-class city and organization, but Robbie was still upset. Then his mother set him straight. "You have to believe it's for the best," she told him. When Robbie fretted about the house he owned, she said, "Forget the house. That's past." The important thing was to look ahead, to go to Toronto and do his best for his new team.

CHAPTER 5
World Series Rings

L ooking back on the trade that took him from San Diego to Toronto, a mature, experienced Roberto Alomar said, "In life you have to take everything the way it comes in a positive way. You cannot take it too personally. Sometimes a change can make you a better player."

But at the time, he admits, it shocked him. "I didn't know where I was going."

He went to Toronto in December 1990 for a card show and ran into more snow than he had ever seen. Taking batting practice amid snow flurries was one thing, but this was an all-out blizzard. He got out of there on the first plane that could take him to sunny Puerto Rico.

When Alomar reported to the Blue Jays' spring training camp in Dunedin, Florida, in 1991, the only player he knew was Joe Carter, who had been traded with him. To Roberto, 23, the 31-year-old Carter became like a big brother. Carter called him "Bebe."

The Blue Jays, born in 1977, had built a winning team after their early struggles as a new franchise. They had won the AL East twice and just missed three times since 1985, but they had yet to make it to the World Series. They hoped the addition of Alomar, Carter, and center fielder Devon White would put them over the top.

The Toronto SkyDome, opened in June 1989, included a 348-room hotel, with 70 rooms overlooking the diamond, and a huge retractable roof. Like several of the players, the unmarried Alomar lived in the hotel. He had a big room with two TVs, room service, many restaurants to choose from, and no traffic to battle to get to the clubhouse. The hotel staff treated him like one of the family. They protected him from stalkers, screened his calls, helped him with his fan mail, and provided friendly ears when he had a problem or just wanted to talk.

People who worked at the hotel got to know the shy, private Robbie. They knew him as a warmhearted, generous young man who sang Spanish songs and danced about his room, and who was more at ease with kids than adult strangers.

It takes time for any player who changes leagues to adjust to the different ballparks, pitchers, and umpires. For Alomar, once around the league was all it took. In May he began stealing bases, launched a 15-game hitting streak, and had 14 extra-base hits, including home runs from both sides of the plate in one game. The Blue Jays went into first place in the AL East on June 3 and stayed there, fending off late threats by Detroit and Boston.

While anticipating his first playoff experience, Roberto's personal highlight was his and Sandy's election by the fans to the All-Star team. The game was played in the SkyDome, and for the first time Alomar realized how Toronto fans had taken him to their hearts.

"When I was introduced they gave me such a long, loud ovation, I never expected it," Robbie said.

Sandy hugged him and whispered, "Take it easy. Don't cry. We're on national TV." But Robbie was not one to conceal his sentiments—sadness or joy, heartache or appreciation.

The closeness of the brothers disappeared once the umpire cried, "Play ball." "We are a close family," said Sandy Jr. "But when we are playing we are very competitive. He knows I'll slide into him to break up a double play, and I know if he's trying to score a run, he'll knock me over."

Sandy avoided talking to his brother when Robbie was at bat and he was behind the plate. "I don't want people thinking maybe I'm giving him tip-offs of the signs or something."

They were just as combative off the field. "We play Battleship, Nintendo, backgammon, and Robbie has to win, just as bad as when we were kids."

In what was becoming routine for him, Roberto had a sizzling September that lifted Toronto into the playoffs with confidence that this time it would be different. Most of the other Jays knew what it was like to get this far and lose; for Carter, Alomar, and White, it was their first appearance. But they all shared the disappointment when a weaker Minnesota team eliminated them in five games.

Alomar led both teams at bat with a .474 mark, but losing took the satisfaction out of it. Winning his first Gold Glove for fielding excellence was small comfort.

Spring training in 1992 was different for Alomar. He had signed a three-year contract for $14 million with an option for another year. The money did not change him or the way he played or lived, but it gave him financial security. He knew that an injury could cut short his career at any time, and he was determined to leave the game protected from the kind of financial problems he had seen his father endure.

Toronto had made two key additions over the winter: pitcher Jack Morris and outfielder Dave Winfield, a 20-year veteran who had played with Roberto's father. As the designated hitter, Winfield kept the bench alert and vocally supported everybody's efforts. He led the team meetings, when players talked over problems and resolved differences, sometimes fighting among themselves, without the manager or coaches in the room. Winfield also conducted the kangaroo court, a fun game in which players paid small fines for things like failing to advance a runner or missing a sign.

"I learned a lot from Winfield," Roberto said, "about baseball and people and life."

The 1992 All-Star Game took Roberto back to San Diego for the first time since he had been traded, and once again it was an Alomar family reunion. Both brothers were elected to the American League team. Roberto invited his old friend and mentor from Salinas, Nestor Pabon, and his wife as his guests at the game. Roberto thrilled the crowd by stealing second and third after singling in the second inning.

Alomar—and the Blue Jays—got off to a torrid start in the pennant race. When their pitching slumped and their lead withered to one game in August, they acquired David Cone, the National League's top pitcher, from the Mets. Then they finally silenced their doubters with an ALCS victory over Oakland that put them in their first World Series, facing the Atlanta Braves.

Roberto had just five hits in the six-game series, but three of them were vital to Jays wins. After losing the opener in Atlanta, the Jays were down 4-2 in Game 2 when Alomar doubled in the eighth and scored on Winfield's hit to bring them within one run. It set the stage for Ed Sprague's two-run homer in the ninth that evened the Series.

The action shifted to the SkyDome on October 20 for the first World Series game played outside the United States. The score was 2-2 when Alomar led off the bottom of the ninth with a single. He stole second. Winfield bunted him to third, and Alomar scored the winning run on Candy Maldonado's hit.

The Alomar brothers were often united at All-Star games. In this July 1991 photo, Roberto (left) of the Toronto Blue Jays and Sandy Jr. (right) of the Cleveland Indians stand together prior to the American League workout in preparation for the All-Star game the following day.

Toronto led 3 games to 2 when they returned to Atlanta for Game 6. The score was 2-2 after nine innings. In the 11th, Devon White was hit by a pitch and walked. Alomar singled him to second. With two outs, it was appropriate that Dave Winfield brought them both home with a double for a 4-2 lead. Atlanta scored once in the 11th. Toronto's 4-3 win brought the World Championship to Canada for the first time.

Alomar believed the Blue Jays had won with their defense. In Game 3 Devon White had climbed the SkyDome wall to haul down David Justice's drive with two men on base, then whirled and threw to the infield for what looked like a triple play. The umpire ruled that one runner had eluded a tag, and the double play was all that counted.

In Game 6 Atlanta shortstop Jeff Blauser hit a hard drive up the middle. Roberto broke with the crack of the bat, leaped to his right and snared it, landed, and threw to first from his knees. And the 41-year-old Winfield robbed Ron Gant of an extra-base hit with a sliding catch in right field that preserved a 2-1 lead.

"The defense has always been denied the credit that it deserves," Alomar said. "People talk about hitting all the time. But you win more games with the glove than the bat."

The celebration in Canada was more than equaled by the revelry in Puerto Rico. When the last out was made, a caravan of cars wound through Salinas, blowing horns and waking the few who tried to sleep that night.

In the Toronto clubhouse Roberto cherished the moment when Dave Winfield, who had waited 20 years for this ultimate triumph, said to him, "You're one of the best players I've ever seen."

Toronto general manager Pat Gillick did not stand pat in 1993. Dave Winfield departed; they replaced him with another leader and supreme hitter, Paul Molitor. Pitcher David Cone was gone; they signed Dave Stewart, an intense competitor who had beaten the Jays twice in the 1989 ALCS. In mid-season they added base-stealing leader Rickey Henderson. When shortstop Dick Schofield broke his arm, they secured Tony Fernandez.

Roberto Alomar was now The Man, the fans' favorite, in Toronto. He enjoyed the role, talking to people,

In Toronto, Roberto became a popular player—the fans' favorite. Here he signs his autograph on a baseball card that was lowered to the team dugout.

doing interviews, participating in community activities, and letting people get to know him better.

As a young, single star, Robbie sometimes found it was difficult to know who was a real friend and who was trying to use him, to separate him from his money, or to entice him into drugs and partying and trouble. Robbie learned to walk away from people who spelled trouble, but sometimes they came after him. During a game at the SkyDome in 1995, a young woman he did not know entered the hotel with a gun, intent on shooting him. She was arrested before she could carry out her plan.

Robbie took women out to restaurants and nightclubs. But he was conscious of his reputation and theirs. He was often content to go to the movies or rent some videos and stay in his room, at home or on the road. He liked action movies with Sylvester Stallone, dramas with Robert De Niro or Denzel Washington, and Danny DeVito's comedies.

Sensation-seeking writers struck Robbie for the first time when a Toronto magazine found someone who was willing to say something bad about him. They turned it into a cover story about his personal life, full of things that weren't true, and without ever talking to him. As a result he stopped talking to the media for a while.

These distractions contributed to his and the team's slow start in 1993. But after the All-Star Game—Roberto's fourth—the team started to roll. They spent every day the rest of the way either tied or alone in first place.

When Alomar got hot he sizzled. He put up the highest numbers of his career till then in runs (109), hits (192), home runs (17), RBIs (93), and stolen bases (55) while batting .326. Once he stole third base while the pitcher was issuing an intentional walk, an unheard-of move.

"The pitcher wasn't paying attention to me," he recalled, "so I decided if he doesn't look at me, I would go before he threw the ball. There was only one out. He lobbed the ball to home plate, so I took advantage of the opportunity and made it to third."

Pitching and defense win pennants, but it helped that the Blue Jays had the top three batters in the league in John Olerud, Paul Molitor, and Roberto Alomar, the first time in 100 years that one team had the top three batters.

In the ALCS against the Chicago White Sox, Dave Stewart won two games, this time for the Jays, who took the series in six. Alomar saved most of his offensive fireworks for Game 5, when he reached base all five times he batted with three hits and two walks. He stole four bases in the series.

Their World Series opponents were the Philadelphia Phillies. In the Series opener at Toronto, the score was 4-4 after five, a tie preserved by a spectacular play by Alomar, who ran far to his left and dove through the air to snare a blooper behind first base off the bat of Lenny Dykstra. The Jays went on to an 8-5 win.

But the next day Roberto contributed to a loss with a rare base-running mistake. With two out in the eighth inning, his team trailing 6-4, Roberto drew a walk. He stole second on Phillies reliever Mitch Williams. Scouts had noticed that when Alomar stole second, he often stole third on the next pitch. They were right. When he took off, Williams was ready for it and threw him out at third.

Baseball strategy says, "Never make the third out trying to steal third base." After the game Alomar admitted, "We all make mistakes. But I will still play my game."

It didn't weigh on his mind for long. He had four hits in Game 3, a 10-3 win at Philadelphia.

Game 4 proved to be not only the pivotal game of the Series, but the longest and wildest in Series history. The Phillies led 14-9 when Alomar began the eighth by grounding out. But the Jays scored 6 runs in the inning and held on to win 15-14 after 4 hours 14 minutes. Toronto now led three games to two. It reminded Alomar of Game 4 of the 1992 ALCS, when his ninth-inning home run had tied it and led to a three-games-to-one advantage over Oakland. And, as had happened then, the Jays lost the next game, the Phillies' Curt Schilling blanking them 2-0.

Back home in the SkyDome for Game 6, Toronto took an early 5-1 lead behind Stewart, the game's top-money pitcher. But the Phils struck for five runs in the

Roberto, famous for his fielding dives and leaps, performs in game #2 of the 1993 World Series.

seventh to take a 6-5 lead. With Mitch Williams again on the mound in the bottom of the ninth, it looked like Game 7 was on tap. Rickey Henderson walked. Molitor singled. Just as Dave Winfield had delivered the winning blow in '92, this time Joe Carter hit a 2-2 fastball into the left-field stands to win the game and Toronto's second straight World Championship.

Alomar batted .480 in the Series, scored five runs and drove in six. But Paul Molitor batted .500 and was everyone's choice for Series MVP. A second World Series ring and a third Gold Glove were enough prizes for the Alomar trophy cabinet for one year.

After the celebrations, Roberto went home to Salinas. Although he would produce even higher numbers in later years, he considered 1993 his best season, "because what I did helped my team win."

Alomar had not played winter ball for three years. His father was managing the Ponce team in the Puerto Rico Winter League. His brother was the catcher. Roberto decided to join them. He wanted to work on a few things. One trait of the greatest players is that they are always working on something to improve their game.

One day in December he tried to stretch a single, slid awkwardly into second base, and broke his ankle. It was the kind of accident that makes team officials lose sleep when their big-league stars insist on playing winter ball. But Alomar was undeterred.

"I was born to play baseball, and that's what I'm doing. I love this game. Whenever I retire from it, I'm going to miss it. So why not enjoy it when you have the chance?"

CHAPTER 6
Uprooted Again

The Toronto Blue Jays had no chance to win their third straight World Series in 1994 because there was no World Series that year. Disagreements between club owners and players led to a players' strike that ended the season in August.

But it was unlikely that the Jays would have made it anyhow. The departure of David Cone and Dave Winfield and injuries to key pitchers hobbled them all year. They brought Cone back in 1995 and opened the season with optimism. They still had the nucleus of their 1992–93 champion team: Alomar, Olerud, Carter, Molitor, and White. Then a wave of injuries swept over most of the pitching staff and the team gradually sank into the cellar.

The record books show a typical Alomar season: .300 batting average, American League records for second basemen of 104 consecutive games and 484 total chances without an error; All-Star honors; Gold Glove. But the stats do not tell the whole story.

Hailed by the club president as the best player in the game in April, Alomar wound up being criticized by the new general manager, Gord Ash; ripped by the media; and booed by his once adoring fans by season's end.

It began when the team's front office decided that the 1995 season was a lost cause and traded Cone, their best pitcher, to the Yankees on July 28 for three minor-leaguers. To Alomar, giving up before an at-bat or a game or a season was over was unthinkable. In protest he sat out the next game, a move that even his supporters thought may have been an error in judgment. Roberto was in the last year of his contract, and the Jays were making no serious effort to re-sign him. Often when a team has a player who will be a free agent at the end of the year, they trade him for three or four young players to help them rebuild, rather than lose the player and get nothing in return. With that in mind, Alomar suggested to the press that the Jays could do that with him if they did not intend to keep him. The writers twisted his comment, making it sound as if Alomar wanted to be traded immediately.

"I never said that I wanted to be traded," he later explained. "They made it sound like I said, 'Trade me now, I want out of here.' And the fans believed what they read in the papers. When I stood out on the field in Toronto and heard them booing me, I knew they didn't understand or know what the truth was. I hadn't said anything like what the writers wrote. But I could do nothing about it, and I learned how the media is."

It got worse. The Jays made a halfhearted attempt to re-sign him, offering him less than what he was earning at the time. To cover themselves with the fans, the front office put him down to the media, criticizing his attitude and lack of leadership.

Joe Carter knew the real Alomar. "It wasn't justifiable," he said. "They picked his whole season apart because he hadn't signed, and it was almost like he had worn out his welcome. When you're out there busting your tail and playing your hardest and people don't appreciate it, it makes it seem like, 'What's the use?' . . . It's hard when you've done so much for a team and a city and then you just get ripped every which way but loose, and you wonder where all the loyalty is."

Robbie had outgrown his sulking ways when things didn't go his way. But the situation had taken its toll. One day, with his father looking on, Robbie says, "We were taking infield and I wasn't paying much attention. My father said, 'If you don't want to take [ground balls], don't do it. But don't show yourself up.' He got my attention. I always respect his advice."

Then things got even uglier. Alomar's back was bothering him, and he sat out the last three games, including fan appreciation day. A few players grumbled privately that he was "faking" to preserve his .300 batting average. Paul Molitor was not among them.

"I played with him for three years.," Molitor said. "The way he plays, with his aggressiveness and the way he slides, he gets beat up out there. I'd seen him go out in 1993 when he was struggling to get himself prepared to play, not only play but produce, when he was hurting, to help his squad win. Those last few games in '95 were meaningless in the standings. If a guy feels he might be jeopardizing something in games that don't have a lot of significance, I'm not going to complain."

The media hit Alomar like a tornado. The boos shook the SkyDome. His brother Sandy had a different view of the fans' reaction. "When the fans are attached to you and they see you might leave, they take exception to that. I would make those boos into something positive. It means they really care about you and you're breaking their heart by leaving. That's the way I see it."

Robbie did not want to leave Toronto. He liked the fans, the city, his teammates, and his living arrangement. But he believed that if the Jays really wanted to keep him, they would not have waited to make an offer until the end of the season when other teams would be bidding for him.

And he resented their tactics of making him out to be greedy and flawed just to try to get him cheaper.

Alomar went home and played winter ball for the San Juan Senadores, coached and then managed by his father. Robbie's .362 average led the league, as his father had done in 1970–71. Only the Cepeda father and son, Pedro and Orlando, had accomplished that family feat almost 40 years earlier.

"It's a big honor for our family," Roberto said.

But his treatment in Toronto still rankled the sensitive Alomar. The following spring he told a Toronto writer, "I'm still upset. After I gave all those years to Toronto, the media tried to put me down, the same way they did with [other players]"—and as they would later do to Joe Carter and Cito Gaston. Alomar was also angry that the general manager had continued to criticize him publicly after the season, turning the fans further against him.

During the winter Alomar attracted plenty of interest from other teams, including a $9 million offer to play in Japan, which he quickly rejected. He preferred to play for less in the major leagues. Alomar's agent put a high price tag on his star second baseman, who wanted him to sign with a team that had a chance to win it all.

Nobody was more avid in pursuing Alomar than Pat Gillick, who had admired him since Robbie's high-school days. Gillick was now the general manager of the Baltimore Orioles. The Orioles had finished third in 1995 and were looking to build a winner. They had hired former Orioles star Davey Johnson as their manager. Johnson had the highest winning percentage of any active manager.

The negotiations with Alomar went up and down like a roller coaster. At one point Gillick all but gave up the chase.

On December 22, Davey Johnson was in the dentist's chair in Florida, the drill poised for action above his open mouth, when his cell phone beeped. It was Pat Gillick calling.

"You've got yourself an all-star second baseman," he said. Alomar had signed a three-year contract. Johnson felt no pain for the rest of his stay in the chair.

"I never expected to play alongside one of the legends of baseball, Cal Ripken," Alomar said at the time. "It's going to be like a dream come true for me."

A smiling Alomar reveals his enthusiasm over his new contract with the Baltimore Orioles.

CHAPTER 7
Gold Gloves and More Boos

C al Ripken Jr. and Roberto Alomar came from simi-
lar baseball backgrounds. Each had traveled every
summer to wherever his father was playing or managing.
Ripken's father, Cal Sr., was a minor-league manager, then
a coach for the Baltimore Orioles. Robbie and Cal Jr. grew
up in ballparks and clubhouses, absorbing the attitudes and
the ways that big-leaguers carried themselves, how they
honed their bats and broke in their gloves, the pranks and
lingo, the joys and frustrations of the game. As a result,
when they broke in, they were more advanced as profes-
sionals than the other rookies.

Both also had something that cannot be taught—
baseball instincts. "You need talent to play this game,"

*Left to right: Roberto
Alomar, Cal Ripken, Jr.,
Rafael Palmeiro*

Alomar once said, "but you have to have the intelligence, too."

Roberto routinely fielded ground balls behind second base, leaping in the air, twisting his body, and lobbing a soft but on-time throw to first. He ran down bloopers on the outfield grass and threw men out from his knees. He scooped up grounders near second base and shoveled the ball to the shortstop in one motion. He got to slow-hit balls to his left and flipped them from the glove to the first baseman. If a man on first was running with the pitch, and the batter hit one up the middle, Alomar might pick it up beyond the bag and flip it behind his back if that was the only way he had a chance of getting the force.

In one game a fast runner on first took off with the pitch. The batter hit a grounder right at Alomar, who saw he had no chance to get the man at second if he took the ball out of his glove and threw it. Most second basemen would concede the base to the runner and throw to first in that situation. Not Alomar. He gloved the ball and flipped it from the glove to the shortstop in one motion, and the runner was out.

These were not improvised plays to Alomar. He practiced all of them during infield drills before every game until they became routine moves. Those who watched him taking grounders during batting practice saw him scoop and flip the ball sideways, behind his back, between his legs. And he looked like a man having fun while working.

Roberto routinely fielded ground balls, leaped in the air, and threw out baserunners from any position.

49

"The biggest part of my game is fielding," says Alomar.

Asked what he enjoyed most in baseball, he smiled and replied, "A play on the defense where I throw myself headfirst onto the grass to trap the ball and get the out, a play that annoys the hitter. The biggest part of my game is fielding."

Alomar told a writer from Puerto Rico, "Spring training is important. You have to experiment to get to your best form.'"

"This year is a very special one, though, because I have had to get used to new players, but actually it's been a lot easier than I thought," he said.

In addition to adjusting to a new shortstop in Cal Ripken, Alomar had to get to know the other infielders. To his left was the catlike Rafael Palmeiro. "With Raffy, I need to know whether he is better going to his right or left. If I learn he is better going to his right, I can play farther over toward second. If he's better to his left, I have to get closer to him."

At third base was B.J. Surhoff, who quickly learned to expect anything at any time from Alomar. On April 17, 1996, at Camden Yards, the Orioles and Red Sox were tied 5-5 in the ninth. With one out, Boston's John Valentin hit a triple. The Orioles infield moved in as slugger Mo Vaughn waved his bat. Valentin took a short lead off third. Vaughn hit a sharp grounder to Alomar. Valentin took one step toward home, then stopped, seeing he had no chance to score. Everybody in the ballpark expected Alomar to toss the ball to first for the easy out on Vaughn. Instead he rifled the ball to third, where Surhoff put the tag on the surprised Valentin as he scrambled back to the bag.

"Most infielders at any position would not make that play," Surhoff said. "They would look the man back and throw to first for the easy out. But Alomar is not afraid to fail or make a mistake. And that's the key to his greatness. He trusts his instincts and abilities. He knows where he's going to throw before he gets the ball, but if he sees an opportunity somewhere else on the bases, in a split second, even in midair, he'll switch and throw to a different base."

Robbie's bat played as big a role in the Orioles' 11-2 start as his glove. From opening day the switch-hitter had been in the zone at the plate. "Everything you hit seems to fall in," he said, explaining the zone. "Every ground ball finds a hole. If you get jammed, there goes a bloop hit. Every pitch seems to hang. You're seeing the ball good and swinging the bat good."

He ran up a 22-game hitting streak and was batting .410 in early June, with 75 hits in the first 45 games. Orioles manager Davey Johnson said, "He has the knack for seeing what needs to be done and doing it. Whatever we need, he gives it to us—single, double, home run, stolen base, great defensive play—he just does it like it's no problem at all."

Alomar went on to put up the best numbers of his career. He set a team record of 132 runs scored, tied the Orioles highest-ever batting average at .328, and set career highs in hits, walks, doubles, home runs, and runs batted in. He won his sixth straight Gold Glove, made his seventh straight All-Star Game, and was named best base runner, best bunter, and second-best hitter in an American League poll.

But this year was destined to be remembered for none of that.

The Yankees had won the AL East and the Orioles went into the last series of the season against Toronto battling the Seattle Mariners for the wild-card spot in the playoffs. They lost the first of a four-game finale at Toronto on September 26, 3-2.

On Friday night, September 27, right-hander Paul Quantrill started the game by striking out Orioles leadoff batter Brady Anderson. Batting second, Alomar stepped into the batter's box. Umpire John Hirschbeck was behind the plate. The count went to 2 and 2. Alomar fouled off the next two pitches. Ball 3 made it a full count. Quantrill threw a fastball sinker, down and away. Alomar took it; it looked too far outside to him. Hirschbeck thought otherwise and rang him up.

"That was no strike," Alomar said to the umpire.

"It was a . . . strike," said Hirschbeck.

Alomar started toward the dugout, repeating, "It was not a strike."

As he neared the dugout he heard Hirschbeck yell, "One more word out of you and you're out of the game."

"Okay, let's just get on with the game," Alomar said from the dugout. But he doubted the umpire heard him, the crowd was raising such a clamor.

Whatever the umpire thought he heard, his right arm swept through the air and Alomar was ejected from the game.

Angered, Roberto bounded out of the dugout. "Why did you throw me out of the game?" he demanded. "What did I do? All I said was let's go on with the game. Nothing wrong with that."

Hirschbeck moved toward him as the coaches and Johnson restrained Alomar, pinning his arms to his sides.

"Get out of here," the ump barked, "you . . . spic."

To a Latino, that word is disparaging, offensive, and inflammatory. Furious, Alomar lost his head. Unable to move his arms, he spit in Hirschbeck's face.

Smelling the makings of a spectacular furor, the media pounced on Alomar, denouncing him as a disgrace to the grand old game and to the youth of the nation. Immediately after the game hordes of writers and TV cameramen swarmed around him. Whatever he said, they scurried to the umpires' dressing room to repeat it. When Hirschbeck took exception to something Alomar was quoted as saying, the umpire tried to fight his way into the clubhouse, threatening to kill Alomar.

The instant he had spit, Roberto knew he had made a mistake. Even though he felt he had been unfairly provoked, he took the blame for the way he reacted and made no excuses. He apologized publicly, but that didn't satisfy

Umpire John Hirschbeck (left), Roberto Alomar (center), and manager Davey Johnson (right) argue over Hirschbeck's bad call.

the wolves of the press. They criticized him for asking the Orioles to help him prepare his statement of apology; Roberto thought his command of English was inadequate to word it properly without help.

Puerto Rican baseball broadcaster Luis Mayoral was not surprised at the way Alomar was treated. "To many in the media it's easy to get on a player from another country who does not master English. Hispanics are easy targets. The media know that they can write what they want and look good in front of their people, and the guy who does not know English so good cannot counterattack."

The next day, before 36,316 howling, booing Toronto fans who had once adored him, Roberto hit the game-winning home run in the 10th inning to clinch the wild card and the Orioles' first playoff appearance in 13 years.

The league president ultimately suspended Alomar for five games, to be served at the start of the 1997 season so that he would not miss the playoffs. The umpires were furious about the delayed sentence. They considered the penalty too little and too late and threatened to strike during the playoffs. Robbie apologized to Hirschbeck and donated $50,000 to Johns Hopkins for research into Lou Gehrig's disease that Hirschbeck's son had.

As always, Roberto turned to his family for support. "He knows how hurt our family was and that was the worst part for him," his father said later. "People who are parents know when their kid has just made a mistake and he is really not that kind of kid. Roberto is a calm, respectful person. But people don't know him. The umpire said something that he considered an insult.

"I told him everybody makes mistakes and he should learn from it and understand that he would have to be strong because he was going to have to face fans booing and screaming at him. 'Keep your head up,' I told him."

If anything, the storm motivated him to play harder. The Orioles faced the defending AL champion Cleveland Indians in the division series. In the final game, Alomar tied it in the ninth with a two-out, two-strike single, then won it with a home run in the 12th. But they lost the ALCS to the Yankees in five games.

Roberto went home to Puerto Rico. "In Puerto Rico," said Luis Mayoral, "the people's first reaction to the Hirschbeck incident was, 'Wow, Roberto shouldn't have done that.' But they knew the character of the Alomar family and took it for what it was: a mistake in the heat of the moment. They would have preferred that it didn't happen, but they moved on and put it behind them."

Sandy Jr. said, "Robbie never had problems like that. He made a mistake. He apologized. We're human beings; we all make mistakes. Those people who boo him, do they ever look at themselves in the mirror and say, 'I'm a perfect person?'"

But Robbie's mistake had been made in front of millions of people, an audience of witnesses that grew with each of the countless television replays of the event. As the hurricane continued to gather intensity, however, the man in the eye of the storm remained calm.

"My mom says we are all human beings," Roberto said. "If they want to crucify me they can go ahead and do it. But I'm going to survive and play my game."

CHAPTER 8
Fulfilling the Dream

The Baltimore Orioles went wire to wire in first place in the AL East in 1997. But for Roberto Alomar it was the roughest ride of his life. It began and ended in pain. And he was never allowed to put the run-in with umpire John Hirschbeck behind him.

Roberto had another adjustment to make in 1997. When he had signed with the Orioles, he had looked forward to playing alongside Cal Ripken Jr. at shortstop for at least three years. But the Orioles switched the aging iron man to third base that spring, after signing Mike Bordick to play short.

Earlier in his career Roberto had been upset with the constantly changing shortstops he was teamed with, but he had learned to adjust quickly. "My dad always told me, 'As long as you communicate and do your job and he does his, it doesn't matter who's there.' It's not such a big deal that you need a year to know somebody."

The most important part of communication was in making the double play. "That's one of the toughest plays for a second baseman. You can't see the runner coming down from first at you. I always want the ball thrown to my right hand or shoulder, so I can get rid of it quickly. But I may want it behind the base or in front of it, depending on how fast the runners are. I want to avoid the sliding runner by staying behind the base if I can. But either way I don't want a bad throw or any surprises while I'm pivoting on my left leg at the same time I'm getting ready to throw. It's a busy few seconds and communication is the key to making it work."

Alomar's style of play made another bit of preparation necessary. "I told Bordick to be ready whenever I got the ball behind the bag. I might flip it to him to throw to first base, since he has a better view of the runner. I didn't want to catch him off guard."

Alomar was hampered by a sprained ankle he suffered in a charity basketball game before spring training. He remained in Florida when the season opened, serving his five-day suspension and getting his ankle in shape. The press had him gambling on the beach and enjoying a vacation, but the truth was that he would rather have been healthy and with the team.

When he got back into the lineup, it didn't take him long to make an impact. He hit three home runs in one game at Oriole Park.

The media continued to dog him with speculation about what would happen the first time Hirschbeck umpired at an Orioles game. Roberto refused to talk about it. He would handle it in his own way.

The meeting occurred on April 22. When the Orioles ran onto the field to start the game, Hirschbeck was stationed at first base. On his way out to his position, Alomar veered toward first, stopped, shook hands with the umpire, spoke a few words, and continued on. Both men wished to put it behind them, but nobody would let them. Cal Ripken observed, "[Alomar's] going to pay for that mistake for the rest of his career."

And so it seemed. Away from home, fans booed him every time he came up to bat or his name was announced. And in every city, broadcasters' tongues and television replays rolled on incessantly. Reporters clung to the story like leeches. They pestered him with the same questions over and over. Alomar tried to put an end to it. "I made a mistake," he said. "I paid for it. I apologized. Let's move on."

At the same time they were booing him, the fans were voting for him on their All-Star ballots. They knew he was the best second baseman in the game. And they had to admit that he remained the best in spite of the rough time they were giving him. He never let it get him down or deprive him of having fun on the field. If anything, it made him more determined to work even harder. He actually hit better on the road than at home.

There were other injuries and controversies. In May he tore a muscle in his left shoulder and was unable to bat from the right side for the rest of the year.

Roberto's mother could not be in Cleveland to see her sons in the 1997 All-Star Game, where Sandy Jr. won MVP honors. Grandmother Toni was ill and needed care. The Orioles had an exhibition game with their Rochester farm team on July 10, following the All-Star Game. Grandma Toni died on July 7, and Roberto wanted to go to the funeral. Club rules said that everybody had to be there for an exhibition game or call in with the reason for their absence. Robbie tried to get a flight to Puerto Rico but did not make it to the funeral. He did not show up for the game, nor did he call to notify the team.

"When he didn't call and he didn't show up, he broke the rules," said Orioles general manager Pat Gillick. "The rules applied to everybody and had to be enforced for everybody. So he left the manager with no alternative but to fine him."

The $10,500 fine imposed by manager Davey Johnson set off another storm. The club owner and the Major League Players Association got involved, both in Alomar's defense. The fine was never collected.

On July 27 Alomar put down a sacrifice bunt, ran hard to try to turn it into a hit, and pulled up limping at first base. He had pulled a groin muscle and went on the shelf for four weeks.

"When you play hard you're going to get hurt," he reflected. "I was never hurt before. I learned that it can happen to me. It made me grow up. I now knew what it was like to be hurt and what you had to do to come back. It made me tougher."

He came back strong, hitting .500 in the last 19 games of the season to finish at .333.

In the division series the Orioles defeated the Seattle Mariners in four games, twice topping Randy Johnson behind the pitching of Mike Mussina. But they again failed to reach the World Series, losing four games out of six (by one run each) to Cleveland in the ALCS.

A more mature Alomar no longer got angry when he lost. "You do the best you can," he said, "and if you don't win it's acceptable because you did your best. But if you give only 40 or 50 percent and lose, that hurts you the most. If everybody gives 100 percent and does what they can to help the team, then it's acceptable to lose games."

In November Alomar went to Los Angeles for arthroscopic surgery to repair the torn muscle in his left shoulder. It was either that or give up batting right-handed because of the pain.

"I did not know how I would come back from it. But the doctor assured me it was not a big operation and I would be fine if I did what I had to do to rehab."

He went home to Salinas, where he and Sandy Jr. have a two-family home next to their parents' house. Roberto has the upstairs and Sandy's family occupies the ground floor. Their sister lives in a house on the other side of their parents' home.

"During that winter it was tough to sleep in some positions," Roberto said. "I might sleep two or three hours a day. And the exercises were uncomfortable at first. I had to use weights and stretch and massage and learn how to move my arm all over again."

For the 1998 season, the Orioles got off to an 11-2 start under new manager Ray Miller. But then they faded, losing ace pitcher Mike Mussina to two terms on the disabled list, while most of the rest of the pitching staff was sidelined with injuries. The Orioles fell below .500 and out of the pennant race as the Yankees ran away from everybody. By the end of June they needed a telescope to see the leading wild-card contenders, the Boston Red Sox, way ahead of them.

As the All-Star break neared and the Orioles sank farther behind, speculation began about trading some of the year-end free agents like Alomar and Rafael Palmeiro for young prospects. The Orioles had given no signs of interest in re-signing Alomar, who found himself in the same position he had been in with Toronto in 1995. This time he said nothing, but he never knew when he woke up each morning if he would finish that day in an Orioles uniform or somebody else's.

At the All-Star Game in Denver, Roberto's three hits, including a home run, earned him the MVP award his brother had won in 1997. "It was a thrill for my family for me to follow Sandy in winning it," Roberto said. "It was extra special because it was the anniversary of Grandma Toni's passing away."

Roberto continued to play his game, putting the ball in play at a .300-plus clip with his easy swing, waving the

An outstanding switch hitter, Roberto can hit home runs from either side of the plate. His total batting average is an impressive .301.

bat like a magic wand to poke or pull or place the ball according to the pitch and the situation. When he played in his 1,000th American League game on June 3, he qualified as the league's all-time leader among second basemen with a .9868 fielding average. He had made just 64 errors in his eight years in the league.

Alomar's injuries in 1997, which could have hampered or even ended his career, were a wake-up call. "You don't know how long you'll be able to enjoy what you're doing. Things happen on or off the field, in baseball or anything in life. Do something that you love, and enjoy it while you're doing it. That's why I feel so lucky, because I am doing what I love the most."

Dreams have a way of falling short when they are actually fulfilled. They don't always live up to the dreamer's expectations. This has not been true for Roberto Alomar. "Being in the big leagues exceeds anything I anticipated or dreamed. I was born to play baseball, and it is the best thing that has happened in my life. What I have gained I really did not set out to find. I still go out every day with the same enthusiasm. At 30, I know I have to work harder to keep playing. I can't coast or figure I have it made, despite all the Gold Gloves and World Series rings. When you lose a step or your bat's getting slower, that's when you have to work a little harder just to stay where you are.

"I still remember my dad telling me, 'Do your job, whatever you have to do—with the bat or the glove—to help the team win. Pay attention to your own job, not what somebody else is doing or not doing.' No matter how good you are, you are still just one of the team. Everybody is in the same boat."

In late November 1998, Roberto Alomar joined his brother Sandy on the AL Central Championship team, the Cleveland Indians, agreeing to a four-year $30–$32 million contract. His addition was said to give the Indians the strongest and flashiest middle infield in baseball.

Upon moving to his fourth team, Alomar chose not to look or plan ahead. "I think about now, and take life day by day. I don't set a lot of goals for myself; that just puts more pressure on you. And I don't think about how long I might play. That's up to my body. I love this game, but I know there is going to be an end. I don't want to think about it. It's going to be tough, I know, whenever it comes."

MAJOR LEAGUE STATS

Year	Team	G	AB	R	H	2B	3B	HR	RBI	SB	AVG.
1988	SD N	143	545	84	145	24	6	9	41	24	.266
1989		158	623	82	184	27	1	7	56	42	.295
1990		147	586	80	168	27	5	6	60	24	.287
1991	TOR A	161	637	88	188	41	11	9	69	53	.295
1992		152	571	105	177	27	8	8	76	49	.310
1993		153	589	109	192	35	6	17	93	55	.326
1994		107	392	78	120	25	4	8	38	19	.306
1995		130	517	71	155	24	7	13	66	30	.300
1996	BAL A	153	588	132	193	43	4	22	94	17	.328
1997		112	412	64	137	23	2	14	60	9	.333
1998		147	588	86	166	36	1	14	56	18	.282
Totals		1563	6068	979	1825	314	55	127	709	340	.301
World	Series										
1992	T0R	6	24	3	5	1	0	0	0	3	.208
1993		6	25	5	12	2	1	0	6	4	.480
Totals		12	49	8	17	3	1	0	6	7	.347

CHRONOLOGY

1968 Born in Ponce, Puerto Rico, February 5

1985 Signs first professional contract with Caguas in Puerto Rico Winter League
Signs with San Diego scout Luis Rosa, February 16

1986 Leads Class A California League with .346 batting average for Reno

1988 Singles off Nolan Ryan in first major league at-bat April 22
Named to the first of nine consecutive All-Star games

1990 Traded to the Toronto Blue Jays

1991 Wins first Gold Glove award

1992 Toronto wins first World Series

1993 Bats .480 in Toronto's second straight world championship

1996 Signs as free agent with the Baltimore Orioles

1998 Wins seventh Gold Glove award; named MVP of the All-Star game; signs
with the Cleveland Indians

INDEX